TAPAS

Anna Cabrera & Vanessa Murphy

BLASTA

CONTENTS

INTRODUCTION

We met in 2008 and quickly realised that our love for food, wine, sangría, vermouth and all the rest made us a perfect match. We often say it's obvious from our waistlines!

Anna, a native of Barcelona, moved to Ireland in 2001, working in food and beverages in the hotel industry. Vanessa had been working in marketing and business development across a range of sectors and had lived in Spain on and off over the years. It's safe to say that our love of all things Spanish is in our blood.

While there was already a Spanish offering in Ireland, we were missing so many dishes from home and our travels around Spain that the idea of our restaurant, Las Tapas de Lola, was born.

The first thing we did was write our menu. The list was long and full of all our favourites. Over the space of three years, we travelled all over Spain in search of the best version of each dish. There's a story behind each and every one of them – a bar down a quiet street, a chiringuito on a secluded beach. All in the name of research!

Our recipes are the way we love to prepare them. There are thousands of different ways to create so many of these dishes, but that's the joy of Spain – each region, city, village, bar and family has their own version that's been handed down over the years. Hopefully you can now make these your own now too.

Las Tapas de Lola opened in 2013. There are three Lolas in our family: Vanessa's mum, Anna's great-grandmother and Anna's aunt, who had a bar in Badalona, her hometown. We named our newborn Lola, as our hope was to open the doors of our restaurant as we would to our own home. To this day, it's been a pleasure to welcome so many people who have become a part of our Lola family, whether on our team or as customers.

HOW TO SERVE TAPAS

Tapas are the perfect party food and even better icebreakers (great for first dates!). They can be enjoyed at a table or bar or simply as finger food. It's all about sharing. And the best part is that you don't have to commit to one dish – you can sample them all.

Some of the recipes in this book serve four and others serve six, but if you're having a tapas evening for four to six of your friends, we recommend that you choose six or seven recipes and go from there.

When serving tapas, it's best to divide them up over a series of smaller plates across your table rather than serve them in one big pile of albóndigas (meatballs), for instance. This way, you can encourage more chats as your friends pass around and share the dishes.

Many tapas can be made in advance and served when required, which means you have more time to spend with your friends enjoying a vermouth (page 7) or a glass of sangría (page 64).

CAZUELAS

Cazuelas (earthen clay dishes) are typically used throughout Spain when serving tapas. They're sold quite widely now and come in a variety of sizes. We mostly use the 14cm dishes so that we can have an array of them on our table.

Before using your cazuelas, it's important to 'cure' them (as it's called in Spain). We do this to close any potential pores in the clay. This makes them more resistant to heat and temperature changes.

To 'cure' six cazuelas, simply cover them with boiling water and 2 tablespoons of fine sea salt, then soak for 2 hours. You only need to do this once after buying your cazuelas. Once 'cured', you can wash them with hot soapy water or run them through your dishwasher.

Gambas al ajillo

WHITE PLATES

More often than not we use simple white plates, as the colours left behind by the oils infused with pimentón (paprika) are just fabulous. We love taking photos of what's left on the plate as much as what was on it to begin with.

WOODEN BOARDS

We use the traditional circular wooden boards for our pulpo a la gallega (page 26). If you're using boards, whether for the pulpo dish or even a nice cheeseboard, always remember to keep them well-oiled to prevent cracking.

OUR KITCHEN STAPLES

When thinking tapas, there are a few staples that are handy to have in your kitchen. These are the ones we could basically never be without.

FRIDGE/FRESH

Garlic

Some more garlic

Olives

Eggs

Potatoes

Raw cooking chorizo

Black pudding

Jamón ibérico

Tomatoes – the riper, the better

Onions

Red and green peppers

Milk

Bread, both fresh and stale

Fruit for your sangría and vermouth – lemons, oranges, apples, strawberries

Cucumber

Oh, and some more garlic

CUPBOARD

Paprika (sweet and picante)

Cumin

Oregano

Cinnamon

Dried chillies

Olive oil

Sunflower oil

Sherry vinegar

Plain flour

Almonds

Piquillo peppers

Tinned chickpeas

Tinned tomatoes

Wine for cooking (or use leftover unfinished wine, but that's a rarity in our home!)

Tins of conservas (Spanish tinned seafood)

Tins of anchovy-stuffed olives

Tinned tuna

Chocolate

Sea salt – fine, coarse and flakes

Black pepper

OLIVE OIL

Olive oil, both virgin and non-virgin, is always in our cupboard. Just as with wine, there are so many varieties and qualities of oils that it's important to keep trying them until you find the one you love. While many wines improve with time, this is not so with olive oil. It's commonly believed that a good olive oil should be consumed within a year from when it's pressed. We have olive oils for cooking, others for salads, others for dunking bread and some so delish you could nearly drink them. On any given day we might have over six different bottles on the go in our cupboard.

NON-VIRGIN

Non-virgin (often referred to as 'regular') olive oils are made with a blend of cold-pressed olives and processed oils using chemicals and heat. The processing creates a milder flavour than virgin and extra virgin oils and makes them clearer in colour too. We use these oils for frying rather than for dipping or salads.

VIRGIN AND EXTRA VIRGIN

Virgin olive oil is made using pure cold-pressed olives. Unlike 'regular' olive oil, no chemicals or heat are used in the process. Virgin oils are typically extracted from the second pressing of the olives. Extra virgin oils are from the first pressing.

Virgin oils are often described as unrefined as they're not processed using chemicals or heat. They are our preferred go-to oils for dunking, salads and some cooking too.

Each oil can vary in quality, taste and price. Some are nuttier than others, some more peppery too, which is why it's always good to keep tasting.

PIMENTÓN
PAPRIKA

Paprika, known as pimentón in Spain, is a staple in every kitchen throughout the country. We can't imagine our kitchen without it in the cupboard. It's used to add flavour and colour to many a dish, tapa and stew as well as Spain's famous chorizos and morcillas (blood sausages).

Pimentón is a ground spice made from dried larger varieties of red peppers (*Capsicum annuum*). It originated in Mexico and is believed to have been first brought to Spain in the 16th century.

In Spain, there are three key different kinds of pimentón:

- Dulce: Mild, also referred to as sweet.

- Agridulce: Mildly spicy.

- Picante: Spicy.

There is a big difference between dulce (sweet) and picante (spicy). If the package doesn't specifically say it's hot or picante, then it's likely to be the sweet version, so its flavour is all about the smoke rather than spice and smoke.

Just as with wines in Spain, pimentón also carries a DO (Denomination of Origin) status to protect its quality and production. That's how fundamental it is to Spanish cooking.

There are two main regions in Spain producing pimentón, both following the centuries-old method of growing, smoking and grinding the peppers to ensure their DO status.

- La Vera in Extremadura is famous for its smoked pimentón de la Vera. Their peppers are smoked over oak for 10–15 days in specially designed wood and brick smokehouses, giving them their delicious smoky flavour. They typically use three different varieties of peppers: Jaranda, Jariza and Jeromín.

- Murcia is better known for its sweet sun- or air-dried pimentón. They use a sweeter variety of pepper (Bola) that is hand-picked, then dried in the sun or in warm kilns over several days – a very different process to the smoked peppers of La Vera.

We use pimentón to add that smoky flavour to some of our dishes, but also that extra punch too. Its flavour varies from mild to a smoky heat, so its main purpose is to add flavour and colour more than the hot spice of chilli or cayenne.

You'll see it appear in our recipes for pulpo a la gallega (Galician octopus), espinacas con garbanzos (spinach with chickpeas), pincho moruno and our brava sauce, to name just a few. We love the colour it leaves on the plate once the dish has been devoured.

VERMÚT
VERMOUTH

We love all things vermouth. It's enjoyed all over Spain and as a result comes in many different forms.

It's a massive tradition in Anna's family that we've both continued while living in Dublin. When we visit Badalona, Anna's hometown, the joy of vermouth is often referred to locally as vermutillo or vermuteo and there are bars dedicated solely to this fabulous concept.

Typically enjoyed at the weekends before lunch (but midweek too), it's an aperitivo event. In its simplest form, it consists of a glass of red or white vermouth (or a bottle shared among family and friends) served with ice, a slice of lemon (some use orange) and olives stuffed with anchovies as a garnish. Some prefer to sip their vermút with a splash of sifón (gaseosa – soda), which is often served from fantastic vintage siphons.

But the most important part is the food that accompanies this tradition. This mainly comes in the form of conservas (tinned and preserved shellfish) served with a bag of salted crisps and olives stuffed with anchovies. The conservas could be anything from mussels to cockles, razor clams to baby squid, ventresca (tuna belly) to sardines or anchovies – the list is endless and there's something for everyone.

And then there's the sauce. A lot of bars make their own, but many use the sauce from one of our favourite vermút bars, El Espinaler. It's made from vinegar, paprika and a variety of spices and it's used to sprinkle over the berberechos (cockles) or the crisps, for example.

We typically take a crisp, pinch a berberecho (cockle) with a toothpick and away we go. Anna is known to drink the remaining juices from the berberechos mixed with the sauce to complete the experience. Nothing goes to waste.

Nowadays, vermouth is on trend around the world and most independent grocers and many supermarkets stock conservas.

SERVES 4

FOR THE VERMÚT:

1 bottle of red or white vermouth

1 lemon, sliced

olivas rellenas (olives stuffed with anchovies)

toothpicks to pinch 2 olivas to garnish your drinks

FOR THE NIBBLES:

Your choice of conservas depends on what's available, but anything goes:

1 tin of mejillones (mussels)

1 tin of berberechos (cockles)

1 tin of chipirones (baby squid)

1 large bag of patatas fritas (salted crisps)

1 tin of anchovies from Santoña

1 tin of olivas rellenas (olives stuffed with anchovies)

1 bottle of El Espinaler sauce (if you can source it)

FOR THE MAKESHIFT SAUCE IF ALL ELSE FAILS:

200ml white wine vinegar

2 tbsp sweet pimentón (paprika)

1 tsp ground cumin

juice of 1 lemon

1–2 tsp juices from the tinned berberechos (cockles) (optional)

To make your own sauce, put the vinegar and paprika in a bowl and whisk to combine, then add the cumin and lemon juice and whisk again. We love to add a teaspoon or two from the juice of the tinned berberechos (cockles).

You can serve these nibbles straight from the open tins or empty them onto individual plates. We prefer white plates as the colours left behind by the jus of the mejillones (mussels) are just amazing.

If we're at home, we pour the crisps into a bowl. If we're in a vermút bar in Spain, we simply open out the bag like a plate and eat straight from it.

The sauce is lovely sprinkled over the conservas, and sprinkle some over the crisps too.

Crisp, mussel, crisp, cockle, crisp, mussel, anchovy-stuffed olive, crisp, etc., etc., while enjoying a sip or two of vermút. Heaven.

BE PREPARED!

Your friends will love this aperitivo, so it's always a good idea to have an extra bottle (or two) of vermút at the ready.

ALBÓNDIGAS
MEATBALLS

SERVES 4

Albóndigas are a great party food or as a staple at the dinner table with large chunks of sourdough bread to mop up the sauce. Typically made with minced beef, we like to add minced pork for flavour and moisture. A lovely extra, should you have one lying around the house, is to add the bone of a jamón ibérico to the sauce when cooking for added flavour.

1 tsp olive oil

½ small onion (50g)

4 garlic cloves, minced

375g minced beef

375g minced pork

1 large egg

¼ tsp dried oregano

1 tsp fine sea salt

½ tsp ground black pepper

FOR THE SAUCE:

2 tbsp olive oil

1 large Spanish onion, diced

½ red pepper, diced

½ green pepper, diced

4 garlic cloves, minced

40ml red wine

½ tsp dried oregano

1 tsp fine sea salt

a pinch of ground black pepper

2 x 400g tins of chopped tomatoes

½ tsp caster sugar

First, make the sauce. Heat the oil in a saucepan over a medium heat. Add the onion, peppers, garlic, wine, oregano and the salt and pepper. Sweat for 15 minutes, until soft. Stir in the tinned tomatoes and sugar, then simmer on a medium to low heat for 1 hour. Set aside.

Preheat the oven to 180°C (160°C fan).

To make the meatballs, heat the oil in a pan on a low heat. Add the onion and garlic and sweat for about 10 minutes, until cooked. Put to one side to cool.

Put the minced beef, pork, egg, oregano and the salt and pepper in a large bowl, then add the cooled onion and garlic mix. Wearing disposable gloves if preferred, use your hands to combine well. Shape the mix into 40–45g balls (roughly 16 meatballs), then place in a single layer in a baking dish. Depending on the size of your dish, you might need to use more than one to keep the meatballs in only one layer.

Cook in the preheated oven for 18 minutes, then remove the dish from the oven and pour over the sauce. Return to the oven to cook for a further 5 minutes, until the sauce and the meatballs are hot.

To serve, simply pour the meatballs and their sauce into a bowl. A sprinkle of chopped fresh flat-leaf parsley is a nice finish. As a tapa we like to split them up over a few smaller dishes and dot them around the table for people to enjoy.

TRY THIS

Our meatballs are easily frozen for another
day. Just cook them for 20 minutes instead
of 18 and allow to cool, then freeze them
without the sauce.

CROQUETAS DE JAMÓN
HAM CROQUETAS

SERVES 4–6

We love all things croquetas! In Spain there are bars, shops, supermarket aisles, books and even daydreams dedicated solely to the croqueta. They come in all shapes, flavours and sizes but we like to keep them simple. Here we use jamón serrano but you can replace the jamón with practically anything – see the croqueta variations on pages 14–15.

125g butter

½ onion, finely diced

250g serrano ham, minced

160g plain flour, sifted

1 litre warm milk

1 tbsp fine sea salt

2 tsp ground black pepper

1½ tsp ground nutmeg

TO DEEP-FRY THE CROQUETAS:

150g plain flour

4 eggs, whisked

150g fine breadcrumbs

2 litres sunflower or vegetable oil

Melt the butter in a large pot set over a medium heat. Add the onion and cook for 8–10 minutes, until soft, then add the minced serrano ham and the sifted flour, stirring constantly until the flour is golden. Pour in the warm milk and whisk constantly until the mixture starts to thicken. Stir in the salt, pepper and nutmeg, then remove the pot from the heat.

Scrape the mixture out onto a baking tray, cover immediately with cling film and leave to cool, then refrigerate for at least 6 hours (or until the next day).

When you're ready to cook, set up three bowls: one for the flour, one for the whisked eggs and one for the breadcrumbs. Using your hands, shape the croquetas to your desired size (we suggest 6–8cm long). Roll through the flour, then the eggs and finish with the breadcrumbs.

Heat the oil in a deep-fryer to 190°C. If you don't have a deep-fryer, you can use a deep pot but make sure it's no more than half-full of oil (see the note on page 17).

Working in batches, deep-fry the croquetas for about 2 minutes, until golden. Remove with a slotted stainless steel spoon to a plate lined with kitchen paper to remove any excess oil. Croquetas are always served hot, but we've been known to steal them cold from the plate at home!

TRY THESE
CROQUETA VARIATIONS

The joy of croquetas is that you can play around with flavours and ingredients. It's as simple as looking in your fridge and thinking, 'What will I do with my leftover chicken from Sunday?' We've given you a few ideas here but the list is endless – think chicken, prawns, lobster, oxtail, mushrooms, cheese. And remember, you can always make these beauties and freeze them for another day. All you need to do is follow our original croquetas de jamón recipe on page 12 and replace the jamón as noted below.

1 POLLO (CHICKEN)

You may have roasted that chicken at the weekend (or turkey at Christmas) and are wondering what to do with your leftovers. Croquetas are the perfect solution. Simply shred and chop 250g cooked chicken (no skin) as finely as possible and add it to the cooked onion instead of the jamón and take it from there.

2 GAMBAS (PRAWNS)

Finely dice 250g peeled prawns. Add to the pan instead of the jamón and cook for 2 minutes, then add the sifted flour and away you go.

4 SOBRASADA & QUESO AZUL (SOBRASADA & BLUE CHEESE)

Sobrasada is a spreadable sausage from Mallorca in Spain. It can be found in many stores these days. Add 125g sobrasada and 125g blue cheese to the pan instead of the jamón and cook, stirring, for 2 minutes to break them down. Add the sifted flour and take it from there.

3 SETAS (MUSHROOMS)

There are so many fantastic mushrooms available throughout the year and they make a fantabulous veggie croqueta. (We often buy mushrooms and forget about them in the fridge.)

Mushrooms tend to release quite a bit of water when cooked, so to avoid having too much liquid in your croqueta mix, your best bet is to finely chop 400g mushrooms, fry them off in the pan with a pinch of salt, then remove them from the pan with a slotted spoon. Add to the cooked onion instead of the jamón, add the sifted flour and carry on from there.

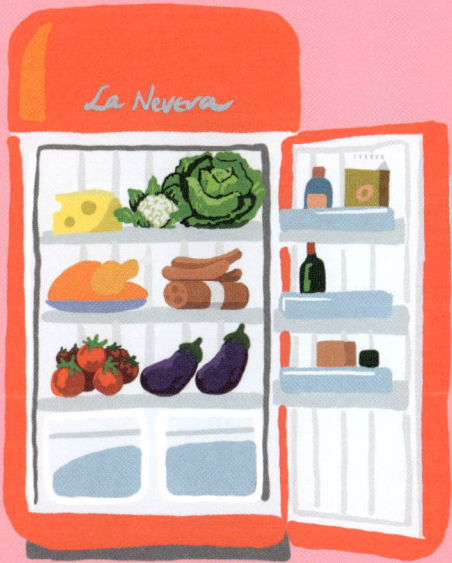

La Nevera

5 REVISIT YOUR FRIDGE & THINK OF WHAT TO TRY NEXT

BOMBITAS DE MORCILLA
BLACK PUDDING BOMBITAS

SERVES 4–6

The bomba de la Barceloneta is a widely loved tapa from Barcelona and greatly loved in Lola. Here we've taken it on a different journey, away from Barcelona and closer to home in Dublin using morcilla (black pudding) instead and replacing the brava and allioli with apple compote and piquillo sauce.

5 large potatoes, unpeeled

1 litre water

fine sea salt and freshly ground black pepper

40ml extra virgin olive oil

½ onion, diced

400g morcilla (Spanish or Irish black pudding), finely chopped

2 tsp sweet paprika

1½ tsp dried oregano

TO DEEP-FRY THE BOMBITAS:

150g plain flour

4 eggs, whisked

150g fine breadcrumbs

2 litres sunflower or vegetable oil

FOR THE APPLE COMPOTE:

2 Bramley or cooking apples, peeled, cored and sliced

4 tsp light brown sugar

75ml white wine

To make the apple compote, put the sliced apples and brown sugar in a frying pan set over a low heat and cook until the sugar melts. Add the wine and cook for 20–30 minutes, until the consistency is like a purée. Set aside to cool.

For the piquillo sauce, heat the oil in a frying pan set over a low heat. Add the onion and salt and cook for roughly 5 minutes, until golden brown. Add the peppers and cook for 5 minutes, then add 150ml liquid from the piquillo jar and cook for 5 minutes more. Blitz with a hand-held blender and set aside.

To make the bombitas, put the whole potatoes, water and 2½ tablespoons salt in a large pot and bring to a boil. Reduce the heat and cook for 20–40 minutes, depending on the size of the potatoes – they need to be cooked through and soft enough to mash. Drain and cool.

Heat the oil in a frying pan set over a low heat. Add the onion and 1 teaspoon salt and cook for roughly 5 minutes, until golden brown. Add the black pudding, sweet paprika and oregano and cook for 10 minutes.

Peel the cooled potatoes and mash them until smooth, then stir in the black pudding and onion mixture. Season to taste.

Set up three bowls: one for the flour, one for the whisked eggs and one for the breadcrumbs. Using your hands, shape the bombitas into bite-sized balls. Roll them through the flour, then the eggs and finish with the breadcrumbs.

FOR THE PIQUILLO SAUCE:

2 tbsp oil

¼ onion, diced

½ tsp fine sea salt

1 small jar of piquillo peppers (6 piquillos)

150ml liquid from the piquillo jar

Heat the oil in a deep-fryer to 190°C. If you don't have a deep-fryer, you can use a deep pot but make sure it's no more than half-full of oil (see the note).

Working in batches, fry the bombitas for about 2 minutes, until golden brown. Remove with a stainless steel slotted spoon to a plate lined with kitchen paper to remove any excess oil.

To serve, put 1 teaspoon of apple compote per bombita on your serving plate or platter. Place the bombitas on the spoonfuls of sauce and dot some piquillo sauce on top.

A NOTE ON DEEP-FRYING

Not everyone has a deep-fryer and a handful of our recipes do require frying. If you don't have one, use a deep pot with enough oil (roughly 2 litres) to cover what you're frying, but make sure your pot is no more than half-full of oil. A stainless steel slotted spoon is perfect for scooping out your bombitas or croquetas (page 12), for example. When scooping something out of the fryer, we always have kitchen roll at the ready to absorb any excess oil.

CHICHARRONES
PORK BELLY

SERVES 4–6

As with so many dishes from Spain, chicharrón (pork belly) comes in many forms – some like ours (crispy, fatty and very salty), some with sauce and others cured and sliced, like the incredibly delicious chicharrón de Chiclana from Cadiz in the south of Spain. We often say that our chicharrones should come with a health warning: fatty, salty and delish. If you'd like to create a thirst for your sangría (see page 64) at your next party, these are certainly the way to do it!

500g pork belly, left whole in one piece

½ tsp whole black peppercorns

1 bay leaf

sunflower or vegetable oil, for deep-frying

FOR THE SEASONING:

25g sea salt flakes, plus extra to serve

a pinch of dried oregano

a pinch of ground cumin

a pinch of sweet paprika

TO SERVE:

½ lemon, cut into quarters

Preheat the oven to 165°C (145°C fan).

To make the seasoning, simply combine all the ingredients together and set aside.

Dot the skin of the pork belly with the peppercorns, then put the whole pork belly in a baking dish. Cover the belly with water and add the bay leaf. Wet a large piece of parchment paper under the cold tap. Cover the pork with the damp paper, then seal the dish with foil.

Cook in the preheated oven for 2½ hours, then transfer the pork belly to a clean baking tray. Cover it again with the damp parchment paper and leave to cool. Cut the cooled pork into bite-sized pieces – usually about 2cm wide and roughly 4cm long. Each belly will vary, but leave nothing to waste.

Heat the oil in a deep-fryer to 190°C. If you don't have a deep-fryer, you can use a deep pot but make sure it's no more than half-full of oil (see the note on page 17). The important thing is that you use enough oil to cover the chicharrones when frying.

Working in batches, deep-fry the pork belly for roughly 3 minutes, until crisp. Use a stainless steel slotted spoon to transfer the pork to a plate lined with kitchen paper to remove any excess oil. In a separate bowl, toss the belly with the seasoning.

Serve on plates with the wedges of lemon. Eat with a squeeze of lemon and a shake of salt. Your heart may stop for a few seconds, but they're delish.

CHORIZO AL VINO BLANCO
CHORIZO IN WHITE WINE

SERVES 4

There are so many ways in which to enjoy chorizo, whether it's on the BBQ or simply fried in a pan. Here, we have a simple classic that's easy to make – just be sure you have enough sourdough to mop up all the cooking juices. We love to serve this dish on a white plate, as the colours that come from the chorizo with the white wine are stunning when left behind.

350g raw cooking chorizo, left whole

1 medium red pepper, sliced (approx. 85g)

1 medium green pepper, sliced (approx. 85g)

300ml white wine

TO SERVE:

plenty of sourdough bread

Heat a dry frying pan over a medium heat. When the pan is hot, add the whole chorizo and cook for 5 minutes to give it some colour. Add the sliced peppers and cook, tossing occasionally, for 4 minutes.

Add the wine to the pan, reduce the heat to low and cook for 25–30 minutes, until the wine has reduced but there's still enough for some bread soakage.

Once it's cooked, cut the chorizo into 2cm pieces in the pan, then it's ready to serve with a large chunk of bread.

CALLOS
TRIPE STEW

SERVES 4

You're guaranteed to get comments from your friends arriving to your home after you've cooked this beauty. The aromas wafting around the house from the spices, chorizo, morcilla, garlic and all the rest will certainly whet their appetites. This is a dunking dish, so be sure to have plenty of soft, doughy sourdough at the ready. It takes some time to prepare, but it's worth every minute.

1kg cow tripe

200g coarse sea salt

100ml white wine vinegar

1 bay leaf

½ tbsp ground black pepper

2 cloves

1 large onion, peeled and left whole

1 large carrot, peeled and left whole

250g raw cooking chorizo (in one piece)

200g raw cooking morcilla (black pudding/blood sausage, in one piece)

200g raw pancetta (we like to buy it as 2 large, long slices from our local butcher)

1 x 400g tin of chickpeas, drained and rinsed

a pinch of fine sea salt

First, you need to clean the tripe. Rub both sides of the tripe with coarse sea salt, then rinse under cold water. Put the tripe in a large deep pot, then cover with cold water and the white wine vinegar. Bring to the boil over a medium heat, then reduce the heat and simmer for 10 minutes. Remove the tripe from the pot and rinse it under cold water again, then pat it dry with kitchen paper. Cut the tripe into pieces roughly 2cm square.

Put the tripe back in your large pot, cover it again with cold water (roughly 2 litres) and add the bay leaf and ground black pepper. Cover and bring to the boil, then reduce the heat and simmer for 1 hour.

Stick the cloves into the whole onion, then add it to the pot along with the carrot, chorizo, morcilla and pancetta (everything left whole). Keep covered and simmer for a further 1½ hours, topping up with another litre of water only if needed. Don't add too much water during the cooking process, as you want a thicker consistency to the stew – you can always add more water towards the end if needs be.

After 1½ hours, remove the bay leaf, onion, carrots, chorizo, morcilla and pancetta and set aside. Some morcillas (black puddings) dissolve into the stew, which is delish too. Leave the tripe in the cooking juices in the pot and set it aside.

Time to make the paste. Chop the onion and carrot that you just took from the pot.

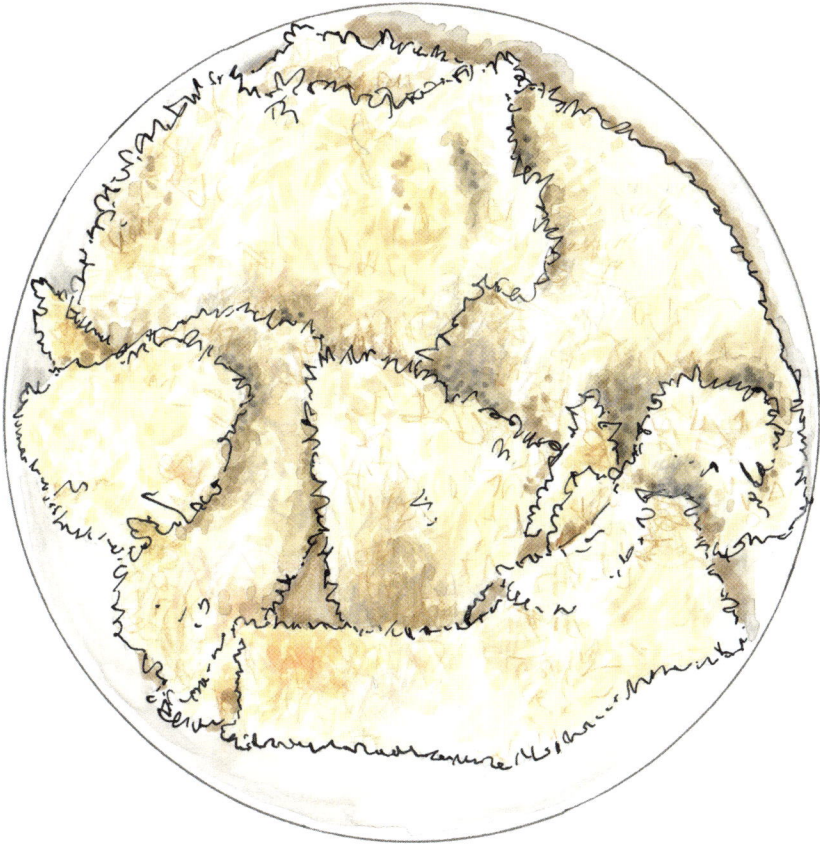

FOR THE PASTE:

100ml extra virgin olive oil

2 garlic cloves, finely chopped

100g tinned tomatoes

1 tbsp ground cumin

½ tbsp sweet paprika

½ tbsp spicy paprika

TO SERVE:

lots of sourdough bread, for dunking

In a separate pan, heat the 100ml olive oil over a medium heat. Add the chopped onion and carrot and the garlic and cook for 5 minutes. Add the tinned tomatoes and cook for a further 5 minutes. Add the cumin and paprikas and stir to combine, then blitz everything with a hand-held blender.

Add the paste to the pot with the tripe and stir to combine, then add the chickpeas to the pot too.

Slice the chorizo, pancetta and morcilla into chunks (roughly 2–3cm) and return them to the pot. Cook on a low heat for 5 minutes. Season to taste with salt, but remember that the chorizo, pancetta and morcilla will have brought salt to the dish already.

Serve with plenty of bread for dunking.

PINCHO MORUNO

MAKES 4 SKEWERS

When Anna was young, she spent time in her cousins' pueblo (village), Venialbo outside Zamora in Spain. Each year Zamora celebrates its city's festivities, with pincho moruno taking centre stage in the bars and on the streets. Every bar holds their recipes close to their heart, never to be shared. Moruno is enjoyed all over Spain, and as with so many Spanish dishes, there are hundreds if not thousands of different recipes for it. But the name moruno (Moorish) tells you everything you need to know about this version – it's full of flavours that have their origins in southern Spain and northern Africa. It can be made with lamb, pork or chicken. The seasoning is also great to use as a rub on meat that's heading to the BBQ.

500g pork steak

juice of ½ lemon

30g sea salt flakes

40ml water

FOR THE MORUNO SEASONING:

1 tbsp fennel seeds

3 tbsp ground cumin

2 tbsp sweet paprika

1½ tbsp dried oregano

1 tbsp ground fennel

1 tbsp cayenne pepper

½ tsp ground cinnamon

TO SERVE:

allioli (page 55)

To make the seasoning, toast the fennel seeds in a pan over a low heat, then crush them in a pestle and mortar. In a bowl, mix the crushed fennel seeds with all the remaining seasoning ingredients and set aside.

Remove all the excess fat and sinew from the pork fillet, then cut it into bite-sized chunks.

Put the lemon juice and sea salt in a bowl and stir until the salt dissolves. Add all the moruno seasoning and the water and mix together, then add the pork and toss to coat. Cover and refrigerate overnight for the best flavour.

If you're using wooden skewers, soak them in water first for a minimum of 20 minutes to prevent them burning when cooking.

To cook, remove the pork from the fridge and put 6–7 pieces on each skewer (you should get four skewers in total). Cook on a hot plancha (flat plate) or griddle pan for best results (or on the BBQ) for 3 minutes on each side, until the pork is cooked through.

Serve with allioli to dip.

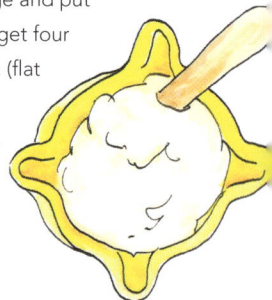

RIÑONES AL JEREZ
SHERRY KIDNEYS

SERVES 4

Kidneys, and all things offal, are very popular throughout Spain. Sherry is used a lot in cooking in Spain and adds a fantastic flavour to this fantabulous kidney dish.

500g lamb kidneys

2 tbsp sherry vinegar (to clean the kidneys)

fine sea salt

4 garlic cloves

1 handful of fresh flat-leaf parsley (keep a sprig or two to garnish)

4 tbsp extra virgin olive oil

1 large Spanish onion, finely diced

2 tbsp sifted plain flour

1 tsp sweet paprika

1 tsp ground black pepper

300ml water

200ml sherry

TO SERVE:

good crusty bread

You can buy kidneys already cleaned from your butcher, but we recommend cleaning them again at home. Cut away all the white excess on the exterior, then place the kidneys in a bowl and cover them with a glass of water, the sherry vinegar and ½ teaspoon salt. Leave to soak for 15 minutes.

Once the 15 minutes are up, put the kidneys straight into a colander to remove any excess jus, then wash them under cold water. Pat dry with kitchen paper and cut into slices or chunks.

While the kidneys are soaking, chop the garlic and parsley with a pinch of salt. Blend together in a pestle and mortar or in an electric blender.

Heat the olive oil in a pan over a medium heat. Add the onion and cook for roughly 5 minutes, until soft. Add the kidneys and stir carefully for 2 minutes. Reduce the heat to low, then add the sifted flour, paprika and pepper. Keep stirring (carefully), then add the water and the picada of garlic and parsley. Cook for 5 minutes.

Just before serving, add the sherry, still on a low heat. Simmer for 5 minutes to reduce the alcohol content.

This is a hearty dish, so we love to serve it in our cazuelas garnished with a sprig of flat-leaf parsley. As with so many of our dishes, this is delish served with chunks of bread to mop it all up.

PULPO
HOW TO COOK AN OCTOPUS

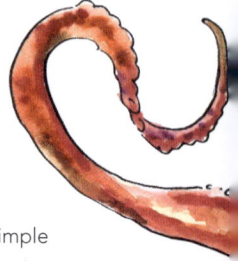

The notion of cooking octopus sends many a cook running, but it's simple enough. You can find whole octopus in many fishmongers or Asian markets these days, mostly frozen. It's believed it's best to freeze the octopus before cooking to break down the fibres. If you fancy a quick cheat, many supermarkets are selling the tentacles cooked already, just in need of plating.

It's worth noting that when you cook an octopus it can lose up to 30–40% of its original weight, so shrinkage is a given.

You'll need 1 x 1.5kg (minimum) octopus, frozen – and remember, if it says it's 1.5kg frozen, this will reduce by almost half upon cooking.

Defrost the octopus under cold running water or in a large bowl in your fridge overnight (as it will lose a lot of water).

Bring 5 litres of water to the boil in a large pot, then add the octopus. The important trick here is to 'scare' the octopus – this means using tongs to dunk the octopus in the boiling water and leaving it in for 5 seconds, then taking it out. Do this three times in total. This is to ensure tender, delicious octopus and that the skin remains on.

After the third time, leave the octopus in the pot, then lower the heat to a simmer. Cook for 30–40 minutes. The amount of time depends on the weight of the (uncooked) octopus – give it 18–20 minutes per kilo. For a 1.5–2kg octopus, 30–40 minutes will be sufficient.

After 30–40 minutes, spear the octopus with a skewer. If it goes in smoothly, the octopus is tender and ready; if not, give it another 5 minutes. Remove from the pot and place on a tray to cool.

PULPO A LA GALLEGA
GALICIAN-STYLE OCTOPUS WITH PAPRIKA & POTATOES

SERVES 4–6

This delicious dish, which comes all the way from Galicia (also known locally as polbo á feira), looks amazing when placed on your table for your guests. Our favourite place to devour it is in the Mercado de Abastos in the centre of Santiago de Compostela while watching the teams bang out board after board after board of pulpo.

1 x 1.5kg octopus, frozen

5 medium Maris Piper potatoes, peeled

1 tsp fine sea salt

2 tsp sweet paprika

1 tsp spicy paprika

2 tsp sea salt flakes

1½ tbsp extra virgin olive oil

Cook the octopus according to the instructions on page 24. When it's cool, cut only the tentacles into slices. Use the head and any leftovers for a potential rice dish.

While the octopus is cooking, put the potatoes in a large pot with the teaspoon of fine sea salt, cover with 1 litre of water and bring to the boil. Reduce the heat and simmer for 20–40 minutes, depending on the size of the potatoes – they need to be cooked through. Drain and cool, then cut into slices.

Mix the two different types of paprika together in a small bowl.

Traditionally this is served on a wooden platter. Using two platters, make a layer of potatoes, then cover that with a layer of sliced octopus. This dish can be prepped and plated, ready to serve later. Simply reheat it in the microwave for 30 seconds at 900 watts, then dust with the paprika mixture, sprinkle the sea salt flakes over the dish and drizzle over the extra virgin olive oil. Now simply wait for the look of glee on your friends' faces.

GAMBAS AL AJILLO
GARLIC & CHILLI PRAWNS

SERVES 4

Gambas al ajillo are all about the garlic, olive oil, chillies and, most importantly, the big chunks of sourdough bread for soaking up the oil once you've devoured the prawns. This is a quick and simple dish that literally cooks in minutes. Our preference is to cook the prawns in a cazuela over a gas flame, but a frying pan will do.

2 dried birds' eye chillies

300ml extra virgin olive oil

4 garlic cloves, chopped

16 shelled prawns

a pinch of sweet paprika

a pinch of fine sea salt

a handful of fresh flat-leaf parsley, chopped

TO SERVE:

sourdough bread, torn or cut into big chunks, for soakage

This all comes together in quick succession, so have everything prepared and ready to go before you start to cook.

First toast the chillies on a hot dry frying pan, then crush them in a pestle and mortar.

Heat the oil in a cazuela or frying pan over a medium heat until it's bubbling. If you're using a small (14cm) cazuela, split the oil (and everything else) evenly between two cazuelas. If you're using a larger frying pan that will accommodate all the prawns, make sure it's wide enough to fit all the prawns in a single layer, not on top of each other.

Add the toasted, crushed chillies and the garlic and cook for 1 minute to infuse the oil. Add the prawns and cook for roughly 90 seconds on each side. There's a trick to cooking prawns: as soon as you think they're nearly done, take the pan off the heat.

Add a pinch of sweet paprika and a pinch of salt. Shake the cazuela or pan, add the parsley and shake it again.

Put the cazuela on a plate and serve it straight to the table or decant into a warmed serving dish or bowl that will take all the oil and prawns straight from the pan. Don't forget the bread!

FRITURA MALAGUEÑA
FRIED FISH PLATTER FROM MÁLAGA

SERVES 4

This is a dish we love to savour when we're down south in Spain, usually with a crisp white wine at a chiringuito on the beach. The south of Spain is known for its fried seafood and this is a great example of it. If the tickle fancies you, it's also lovely served with our allioli (page 55) for dipping.

200g plain flour

a pinch of fine sea salt

250g cod fillet, cut into 12 chunks (approx. 6cm)

185g (approx. 12) squid rings

185g (approx. 12) shelled prawns

120g (approx. 24) squid tentacles (baby squid)

100g whitebait

sunflower or vegetable oil, to deep-fry

TO SERVE:

a pinch of sea salt flakes

½ lemon, cut into wedges

Sift the flour into a bowl and season with a pinch of fine sea salt.

Lightly coat all the seafood in the seasoned flour. Shake off any excess flour and put the seafood in a bowl.

Heat the sunflower or vegetable oil in a deep-fryer to 180°C–190°C (or see the note on page 17 if you don't have a deep-fryer). Working in batches, fry all the seafood for 2–3 minutes, until golden. Transfer to a dish lined with kitchen paper to remove as much oil as possible.

Serve on a plate with a pinch of sea salt flakes and lemon wedges for squeezing over.

BUÑUELOS DE BACALAO
COD FRITTERS

MAKES 20

In Spain we use salted cod that we desalt for 12–24 hours in advance (see the esqueixada recipe on page 46). It's not readily available in Ireland, so we've used regular cod here. If using salted cod, be sure to taste it and mind the amount of salt you use.

400g fresh cod

2 garlic cloves, crushed

a small handful of fresh flat-leaf parsley, chopped

zest of ½ lemon

2 tsp olive oil

100ml full-fat milk

90g plain flour

½ tsp baking powder

1 tsp fine sea salt

1 large egg, beaten

sunflower oil, to deep-fry

Poach the cod in hot gently simmering water for 5 minutes, then drain off the water, tip the cod out onto a plate and allow to cool.

Combine the garlic, parsley, lemon zest, oil and 50ml of the milk together in a large bowl, then blend with a hand-held blender until smooth.

Sift the flour, baking powder and salt into a separate small bowl.

Crumble the cod into the garlic and parsley mixture and stir to combine. Add the egg and stir to combine again, then gradually add the remaining 50ml of milk. Finally, whisk in the flour mixture.

Heat the oil in a deep-fryer to 190°C. If you don't have a deep-fryer, you can use a deep pot but make sure it's no more than half-full of oil (see the note on page 17).

It's all about the scoop and drop into the oil. Using an ice cream scoop or a tablespoon, scoop the mix into roughly 25g pieces (you should get about 20 fritters).

Working In batches of three or four at a time, deep-fry the buñuelos for 3–4 minutes, slowly turning them until golden. Using a slotted stainless steel spoon, transfer to a plate lined with kitchen paper to soak up any excess oil.

Serve hot.

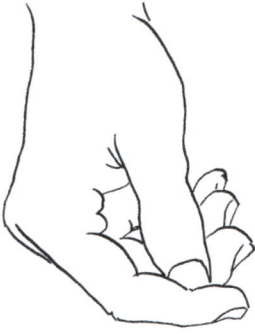

Pulpo a la gallega

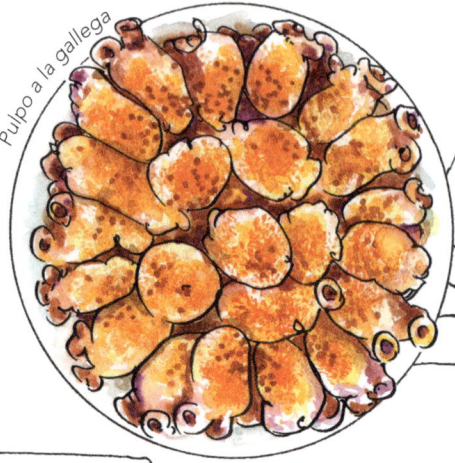

Chicharrones

Pimientos de Padrón

Patatas bravas

Ensaladilla rusa

Pincho moruno

Manchego

PAN
BREAD

A meal without bread in Spain is like a table without legs. No table is ever without bread.

There are an estimated 315 different varieties of bread in Spain. You can understand the Spanish love of bread through two simple facts: (1) standalone bakeries still exist on nearly every street corner and (2) there are six IGPs (Indentificaión Geográfica Protegida, or Protected Geographical Identification) that protect the breads listed below, just like a Designation of Origin (DO) for wine:

- Pan de Cea
- Pan Gallego
- Pan de Cruz de Ciudad Real
- Pan de Alfacar
- Mollete de Antequera
- Pan de páyes (we love to use this for our pa amb tomàquet on page 34)

In addition to the six breads protected by the IGP, there are hundreds more that are simply delicious. Some are fab for mopping, some for toasting, others for cooking.

Bread is so important to Anna's family that when we're home visiting, her dad often gets her up early to head to a village nearby just for the bread from a particular baker. This is serious shopping.

You'll even find a museum in Valladolid dedicated to bread, El Museo del Pan, and a fantastic restaurant in Madrid, Ramón Freixa, that's been using their masa madre for 75 years.

When we opened Las Tapas de Lola back in 2013, we met with a wonderful Spanish woman from the embassy here and her one and only question about the menu was, 'What bread will you have?'

Bread is used throughout the eating experience in Spain, whether it's complementing delicious anchoas (anchovies), cheese and charcuterie as a pre-dinner nibble, as an ingredient in soup (like the salmorejo on page 52) or simply to mop up a delish stew or garlic-infused oils (see the recipes for our callos on page 20 or our gambas al ajillo on page 27). But it appears in desserts too – at Easter, it's used to make delicious torrijas (similar to French toast but on another level).

When it comes to staples, there's nothing more important than bread in Spain.

TOMATES
TOMATOES

Vanessa jokes that you can always spot a Spaniard in a supermarket in Ireland. They stand by the tomatoes, squeezing them, sniffing them – and quite often returning them to their display. Ireland has some of the juiciest tomatoes when they're in season, but we struggle when they're out of season.

We're also limited as to the varieties available in Ireland. It's reckoned that there are more than 10,000 varieties grown around the world and 10% of these are grown in Spain. It's the second most consumed vegetable (or fruit) in Spain after the potato (more on that later – see page 39). The average Spaniard consumes around 12.8 kilos of tomatoes a year!

Most of the tomatoes grown in Spain come from Extremadura and Andalucía, but not simply from there. They are so revered in Spain that there's even a yearly festival in Santa Cruz de Bezana, Cantabria, where they award the best tomato in Spain.

When we're in Spain and cooking at home, here are some of our favourites that we always seek out:

- Raf tomates: Considered to be the pata negra of tomatoes (or in other words, the best of the best).

- Tomates de colgar: Ideal for pa amb tomàquet (page 34) – we may have snuck some of these home in our hand luggage from Spain!

- Rosa de Barbastro: Fab for salads.

- Roma: Great for soups (like the gazpacho on page 50 or the salmorejo on page 52).

When we order tomatoes for our pa amb tomàquet in Las Tapas de Lola, we always ask our suppliers to send us the ripest of the ripe – the ones that a lot of others might return – as they're the best for rubbing over toasted bread or making yum soups too. So if you're shopping outside of Spain and looking for tomatoes for your tapa evening, seek out the ripest ones – they'll usually be the most flavoursome ones too.

PA AMB TOMÀQUET
TOMATO BREAD

SERVES 4

Pa (bread) amb (with) tomàquet (tomato) complements every dish in this book and is one of the basics when we visit home. It's also a ritual in and of itself and is traditional throughout Catalunya (and in different guises all over Spain). The order of things is important. Some love it with allioli too (page 55), others just as it is.

When entertaining, we love to pile all the toasted slices of bread with the whole tomatoes, garlic, olive oil and salt (and allioli if the tickle fancies you) on the board. It makes for great drama on your table. Then everyone can dive in and make their own pa amb tomàquet.

1 pa de pagès (typical in Catalunya) or a sourdough boule – it's important for the slice to be nice and long

2 garlic cloves, unpeeled

2 ripe vine tomatoes (the riper, the better)

a pinch of fine sea salt

your favourite extra virgin olive oil

Preheat the grill.

Slice the bread lengthways so that you get four lovely long slices of bread (one slice per person). Toast on both sides under the grill.

Meanwhile, slice the end (butt) off the garlic cloves, but leave the skins on.

To serve, rub the butt of the raw garlic over the slices of toasted bread. Cut a tomato in half and rub that half over the slice of bread – really mush it in. Discard the tomato once used.

Sprinkle with a pinch of salt. Drizzle with olive oil. Ready to go.

TOP TIP

If you're thinking of using allioli instead of salt and olive oil, we spread the allioli on top of the tomato. DELISH.

TORTILLA DE PATATAS
SPANISH OMELETTE

SERVES 2–4

Tortilla is a staple throughout Spain. This is the traditional tortilla de patatas (omelette with potatoes). In Spain, debate rages among family and friends: with or without onion? Dry or gooey? (We love it with onion and just the perfect level of gooiness.)

It's such a versatile dish too. You can add all sorts of flavours to your tortilla should you wish – spinach, artichokes, the list goes on. It's also lovely served with allioli (page 55) and is best served at room temperature, not straight from the fridge, for optimum flavour.

4 Maris Piper (or waxy) potatoes, peeled and cut into chunks (3cm max)

fine sea salt

olive or sunflower oil

1 medium white onion, chopped or sliced, depending on your preference (we love it sliced)

5 large eggs, beaten

TO SERVE (OPTIONAL):

allioli (page 55)

Rinse the potato chunks in cold water. Drain and pat dry, then season with salt.

Heat the oil in a large frying pan over a low heat (roughly 6cm deep to cover the potatoes). Add the potatoes first, then add the onion straight after and cook until soft, not crispy – usually about 15 minutes.

Using a slotted spoon to drain off any excess oil, transfer the potatoes and onion into a large bowl and season with salt. Stir in the beaten eggs along with another pinch of salt.

Lightly coat the base and sides of a deep, 21cm diameter frying pan in oil, then put the pan over a medium heat. Have a plate that's the same size as your pan handy too.

Pour the egg, potato and onion mixture into the heated pan. Cook on a high heat for 30 seconds if you like it gooey or 1–2 minutes for a firmer tortilla, until you see the sides of the tortilla pulling away from the edges of the pan. Put the plate on top of the pan and carefully flip the tortilla onto the plate, then slide it back into the pan so that the side that was on the bottom of the pan is now on top.

Repeat one more time if you prefer a gooey finish or four times for a firmer tortilla, cooking each side for 15–20 seconds. How long you cook the tortilla for depends on how dry or gooey you like the centre to be – check by pressing the middle of the tortilla.

When you're happy, slide the tortilla onto a plate. When ready to devour, cut into wedges and serve with allioli (if using).

TRY THESE

TORTILLA VARIATIONS

Just as with croquetas and their variations (pages 14–15), you can have lots of fun with your tortillas and they're a fab way to use up what you have in your fridge. There are very few limits to what you can use as an alternative filler to the traditional potato and onion tortilla. We're always amazed at what Anna's mum conjures up in her kitchen from one day to the next!

1 QUESO (CHEESE)

You can use any soft, creamy cheese for this (no rind!). We use Tetilla, a delicious Spanish cheese from Galicia, but you can use Brie or the lovely mild Durrus from West Cork, for example (remember, no rind).

Following the recipe on page 37, once you have the potatoes and onion cooked and mixed in the bowl, microwave 100g of your cheese for 20 seconds, then add it to the bowl along with the eggs and keep following the steps from there. We love this cheese version – nice and gooey.

2 CALABACÍN (COURGETTE)

Substitute 1 large courgette cut into 1cm-thick slices for the potatoes.

3 ESPINACAS (SPINACH)

This is a really simple one. Shred 500g fresh spinach. Heat 1 tablespoon sunflower oil in a frying pan on a high heat. Add the spinach and onion (no potatoes) and cook for roughly 5 minutes, until wilted, then follow the recipe from there.

4 CHORIZO

Using 200g cured chorizo, simply dice it up small and add it to the beaten egg mixture – there are no onions in this delish version.

PATATAS
POTATOES

When people think of potatoes, many think of us Irish and our love of all things spuds – but the Spanish certainly give us a run for our money! It's estimated that Spaniards consume 56kg per capita of potatoes a year (versus 69kg in Ireland). This is well reflected in our restaurant, Las Tapas de Lola, as we order kilos upon kilos upon kilos of potatoes a week.

Many would be surprised to know that potatoes take prominence in the Mediterranean diet. It's the number one ingredient in so many dishes, from oven baked, fried or boiled dishes to stews, salads, omelettes and the thousands of other fantastic recipes throughput Spain. We could dedicate an entire book just to potato recipes from Spain – now there's an idea!

Potatoes are loved so much in Spain due to their versatility in texture, shape, size and flavour – they let our food daydreams run wild.

It's alleged that there are over 7,000 different varieties of potatoes around the world, with Spain producing close to 150 of these. Many would be familiar to the eye when you're shopping, but some are so specific to certain areas that dishes are produced there to complement their potato. One such potato is the negra y bonita from the Canary Islands, which is used to make their delicious papas arrugás (wrinkled potatoes).

We tend to use waxy potatoes for our dishes – like our tortilla (page 37), pulpo a la gallega (page 26), patatas bravas (page 40), ensaladilla rusa (page 48) and bombitas de morcilla (page 16) – that can be sourced very easily in your local market or supermarket. But we have been known to sneak spuds home from Spain in our luggage, just to try them!

PATATAS BRAVAS

SERVES 4

From bar to bar and region to region, patatas bravas come in hundreds of different guises. Some serve them with brava sauce only, while where we hail from, around Barcelona, we like to serve them with both brava and allioli. They're a staple on every tapa menu and always a firm favourite in Las Tapas de Lola. Who can say no to fried potato and delish dipping sauces? Not us!

3 large Maris Piper potatoes (roughly 250–300g), unpeeled

sunflower or vegetable oil, to deep-fry

a large pinch of fine sea salt

TO SERVE:

allioli (page 55)

brava sauce (page 53)

a handful of fresh flat-leaf parsley, finely chopped

Cut the unpeeled potatoes into chunks (roughly 2–3cm). Rinse the potatoes in cold water. Drain and pat dry.

To parcook the potatoes, heat the oil in a deep-fryer to 120°C (or see the note on page 17 if you don't have a deep-fryer). Working in batches if necessary, add the potatoes to the hot oil and cook for 20 minutes. Remove and allow to cool.

When you're ready to serve, heat the oil in the deep-fryer to 190°C this time. Add the parcooked potatoes and deep-fry for about 2 minutes. Transfer to a plate lined with kitchen paper to remove any excess oil, then transfer again into a bowl and toss with a pinch of salt.

To serve, divide the potatoes between a few serving dishes so that they can be spread along the table. On each pile of potatoes, add 2 tablespoons of allioli – one tablespoon on each side – then add 1 tablespoon of the brava sauce in a line between the two spoonfuls of allioli. Garnish it all with a sprinkle of finely chopped parsley.

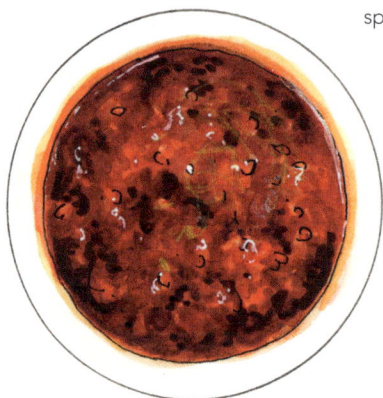

ESPINACAS CON GARBANZOS
SPINACH WITH CHICKPEAS

SERVES 4

There are so many different ways to enjoy spinach in Spain that we could write an entire book just on that, but we particularly love it this way. The inspiration for this recipe comes from one of Sevilla's oldest tapas bars, El Rinconcillo, which recently celebrated its 350th birthday. We keep it purely vegetarian, but we've heard a rumour that when stewing the dish in El Rinconcillo, they add the bone from the jamón for flavour. Delish!

650g spinach, shredded

4 tsp olive oil

¾ tbsp ground cumin

2 tsp sweet paprika

2 tsp fine sea salt

2 x 400g tins of chickpeas, drained and rinsed

TO SERVE:

small slices of sourdough bread, toasted

Bring 1 litre of water to the boil. Add the shredded spinach and cook for 8 minutes, then drain and set aside.

Put a medium-sized pot on a medium heat. Add the oil, cumin and paprika and cook gently for 2 minutes, stirring constantly. Add the spinach and chickpeas and cook for a further 5 minutes, then season with the 2 teaspoons of fine sea salt (or to taste).

Delicious served with small slices of toasted sourdough.

CHAMPIÑONES AL AJILLO
SAUTÉED GARLIC MUSHROOMS

SERVES 4

Simplicity is king with this recipe, which is so quick to make. The twist of picada really makes this dish. A picada is fab to always have in your kitchen for vegetables, salads (like the esqueixada on page 46), fish or meat.

500g button mushrooms

3 tbsp extra virgin olive oil

1 tsp fine sea salt

3 garlic cloves, finely chopped

FOR THE PICADA DE PEREJIL Y AJO (PARSLEY, GARLIC & OLIVE OIL DRESSING):

15g fresh flat-leaf parsley (2 large handfuls)

4 garlic cloves, chopped

300ml extra virgin olive oil

TO SERVE:

toasted sourdough bread

Make the picada before you prepare the mushrooms so that it's ready to serve. If you have a hand-held blender, put all the picada ingredients – parsley, garlic, olive oil – in a bowl and give it all a quick blast, until well combined but not too smooth. Alternatively, use a pestle and mortar.

To prepare the mushrooms, peel them and leave the stalks on. Cut into three slices per mushroom – you don't want them to be too thin.

Heat the extra virgin olive oil in a pan set over a high heat. Add the mushrooms and toss for 2 minutes, then add the salt and toss again. Done!

To serve, divide the mushrooms between two plates. Sprinkle half of the raw chopped garlic over each plate of mushrooms, then sprinkle over 2–3 tablespoons of the picada. Fabulous served with toasted sourdough bread.

PIMIENTOS DE PADRÓN
PADRÓN PEPPERS

SERVES 4

This is such a simple dish to prepare and it looks fab on the table too. Traditionally, we eat the peppers straight off the stalk – no cutlery required, just your fingers.

Pimientos de Padrón take their name from the municipality they come from (Padrón) in the province of A Coruña, Galicia. Some of the best come from Herbón. They're also protected with an EU Protected Designation of Origin (PDO). In recent years they've become so popular that variants are being grown and sold from countries such as Turkey and Morocco. They might look and taste the same, but they don't have the PDO that those from Padrón do.

Some can be spicy, hence the expression 'unos pican otros no' (some bite, others not). It's a kind of Spanish roulette, as we call it. And when they bite, they really bite. We've shed many a tear, but once you recover it's straight back to devouring more.

500ml sunflower or vegetable oil, to fry

350g pimientos de Padrón

1 tbsp sea salt flakes

Heat the oil in a deep pan set over a medium heat. You need enough oil to cover the peppers in a pan, so exactly how much you need depends on the size of your pan. The main thing is that the peppers are completely covered in oil. A mistake that many people make is to use too little oil, which means the blister effect around the peppers is harder to achieve.

So once your oil is nice and hot, add the peppers and fry for 1–1½ minutes, until the skins blister. Remove them from the pan before they turn brown – it's important to retain their beautiful green colour, so a quick fry will suffice. Use a stainless steel slotted spoon to remove them from the pan to a dish lined with kitchen paper to absorb any excess oil.

Plate up straight away, sprinkle over the sea salt flakes and take your chances. Remember: unos pican otros no!

ENSALADA DE PULPO
OCTOPUS SALAD

SERVES 4–6

Our first experience of this simple dish was in a fantastic restaurant on the port in Estepona, Málaga called Restaurante La Escollera that's famous for its pulpo salad – it sells 20–30 kilos of it a day! Heaven. This salad is also a great way to use up any octopus left over from making pulpo a la gallega (page 26), but in that case it might serve fewer people. We're at our happiest having a container of this in the fridge to graze from when we're feeling peckish.

1 x 1.5kg octopus, frozen

2 Spanish onions, roughly chopped

2 large handfuls of fresh flat-leaf parsley, roughly chopped

100ml extra virgin olive oil

2 tsp sea salt flakes

1 tsp freshly squeezed lemon juice

1 tsp white wine vinegar

Cook the octopus according to the instructions on page 24. When it's cool, roughly chop the tentacles – you can use the head for this dish too, but we prefer tentacles only.

Put the chopped octopus in a large bowl with all the other ingredients and toss to combine, then chill in the fridge.

Serve cold straight from the fridge.

TOP TIP

We always have a little parsley oil knocking about (see the recipe for esqueixada on the next page) and it's lovely drizzled over this salad before serving.

ESQUEIXADA
CATALAN SALTED COD SALAD

SERVES 4–6

This is a very typical, and simple, Catalan salad made with salted cod, black olives, tomato and onion. We've kept to the basics, but you can also add chopped red and green peppers, anchovies or even tuna for extra flavours and colour. It's delish straight out of the fridge served with crispy toasted bread – a refreshing addition to your tapa table.

450g salted cod, desalted and finely chopped

1 small Spanish onion, sliced

3 ripe tomatoes, roughly chopped

100g pitted black olives – 50g sliced, 50g left whole

1 tsp cracked black pepper

FOR THE SALAD DRESSING:

25ml extra virgin olive oil

1 tsp sherry vinegar

½ tsp fine sea salt

FOR THE PARSLEY OIL (OPTIONAL):

50ml extra virgin olive oil

10g fresh flat-leaf parsley (without the stalks), chopped, plus a few sprigs to garnish

TO SERVE:

thinly sliced toasted bread

It's possible nowadays to buy salted cod that's been desalted already, but in the event that it's not, soak it in cold water in your fridge for 12–24 hours depending on how salty it is, changing the water every 6–8 hours. Taste to check that it's to your liking, as this will determine when you stop soaking it. The amount of salt can vary from one piece of salted cod to another, so always try a little piece to see how you're getting on.

Whisk together the oil, vinegar and salt for the dressing.

In a large mixing bowl, combine the chopped desalted cod with the onion, tomatoes and sliced black olives (keep the whole ones for garnish at the end). Add the dressing and mix gently to combine, then sprinkle over the cracked black pepper and mix again. Refrigerate for a minimum of 1–2 hours, as this dish is best served cold.

If you're making the parsley oil, use a hand-held blender to combine the extra virgin olive oil and the chopped parsley until fine and smooth.

How you present this dish is up to you. It can be served as a salad plate straight to the kitchen table, or if you decide to be more tapa style and

have moulds in the kitchen, you can individually pack your moulds, then serve onto white plates. Either way, garnish with the whole olives, then finish with a drizzle of the parsley oil (if using) on top and around the bottom of the salad on your dish. Serve with thinly sliced toasted bread.

ENSALADILLA RUSA
RUSSIAN SALAD

SERVES 4

Known familiarly among the Spanish as ensaladilla, this tapa is a certain way to know the quality of the bar you're in. It's a traditional tapa that Vanessa never fails to order when in Spain. We often refer to it as a hug on a plate – total comfort food.

550g potato, diced (Maris Pipers work well)

90g carrots, diced

90g frozen peas (petit pois)

1 egg

200g tuna in sunflower oil, drained of any excess oil

320g mayonnaise

1½ tsp fine sea salt

2 piquillo peppers, sliced into thin strips

15 green olives stuffed with anchovies

TO SERVE:

picos (Spanish mini breadsticks)

Put the potato in a pot, cover with cold water and bring to the boil. Reduce the heat and simmer gently for 10–15 minutes, until completely cooked. Drain well and set aside to cool.

Cook the diced carrots the same way that you did the potato but for only 5–7 minutes.

In a separate pot of boiling water, blanch the frozen peas for 2 minutes, then drain and set aside to cool as well.

Bring a small pot of cold salted water to the boil. Carefully add the egg and boil for 9–10 minutes – the yolk needs to be hard, as it will be grated later. Set aside until it's cool enough to handle, then peel.

Make sure all the vegetables and the tuna are completely drained and dry to avoid watering down the dish, then put them in a large bowl and mix them with the mayonnaise and salt.

To serve, grate the hard-boiled egg. Put the ensaladilla mix in a dish, sprinkle the grated egg on top and garnish with the strips of piquillo pepper and olives. This salad is best served cold straight from the fridge. We love to serve it with picos, Spanish mini breadsticks that can be found in most supermarkets these days.

SOPAS

SOUPS

We're giving you just a small taste of three perfect summer soups, served cold and outrageously refreshing.

The great thing about these soups is that they're simple to make. You can prepare them the day before and refrigerate overnight to use the next day. In fact, they taste even better the next day. You can have fun with your garnishes too. They're fab served in an espresso glass for parties or in a bowl for lunch. During the summer months, we love to have a container of soup in the fridge at home that we dip in and out of.

Some of these soups are denser than others, so quantities will vary. We prefer to serve smaller portions of the ajo blanco and the salmorejo, as they are slightly heavier than the gazpacho – they are nearly a meal in themselves.

They're a perfect way to use up leftovers from the fridge and you can use old bread too, but we use the dough only, never the crust. Enjoy.

GAZPACHO

SERVES 4–6

Gazpacho is a traditional tomato soup from Andalucía that's served cold. It's enjoyed all over Spain, especially in the hot summer months. It's a perfect vegan dish too. Due to its gorgeous colour, we love to serve it in a clear espresso glass as a shot.

1kg ripe tomatoes – the riper, the better

1 small green pepper

1 small red pepper

80g cucumber

40g onion

2 garlic cloves, peeled, though this depends on how much (or how little) you love raw garlic – add it to taste

250ml cold water

80ml sherry vinegar

1 tsp fine sea salt

150ml extra virgin olive oil

TO GARNISH:

1 small red onion, finely diced

1 small green pepper, finely diced

croutons

TOP TIP

This serves four to six as bowls but many more if serving party-style in small clear espresso glasses.

Put all the ingredients except for the oil and the garnishes in a blender. Blend until smooth, then add the oil and blend again for a few seconds. Refrigerate until you're ready to serve – in fact, this tastes even better the next day.

Serve in bowls (or in small cups or glasses) cold from the fridge, with each serving topped with a sprinkle of diced red onion, diced green pepper and croutons.

AJO BLANCO
COLD ALMOND SOUP

SERVES 4–6

This is a delicious summer soup. Typically from Granada and the Málaga region, its main ingredients are crushed almonds, bread and garlic. It's usually served with grapes or a slice of melon to garnish. We love to dunk the grape into it and devour.

150g raw almonds

100g roasted almonds, without skin

75g bread – you can use day-old bread, but use the dough only, not the crust

1 garlic clove, peeled

3 tbsp sherry vinegar

1 tsp fine sea salt

150ml extra virgin olive oil

1 bunch of red grapes

You can soak the almonds overnight in 200ml cold water, but this isn't completely necessary.

However, it *is* necessary to soak the bread in cold water – cover it completely to soak for 2 minutes, then drain.

Put the soaked almonds (and their soaking water) in a blender along with the soaked drained bread, garlic, sherry vinegar and salt. If you've soaked the almonds (and are using the water from same), add another 200ml of water. If you haven't soaked the almonds, add 400ml water.

Blend until smooth, then with the blender still running, slowly add the olive oil little by little. You can add more cold water until you've achieved your desired texture. If you plan to drink it, add more water. If you're using it more as a creamed soup, use less water. Make sure to taste it and add more salt if needed – the more water you add, the more salt it will need.

Refrigerate until you're ready to serve. Just as with the gazpacho (page 50) and salmorejo (page 52), this tastes even better the next day.

Serve cold in four bowls with chopped red grapes on top, or as a shot in six clear espresso glasses with two red grapes skewered on a cocktail stick.

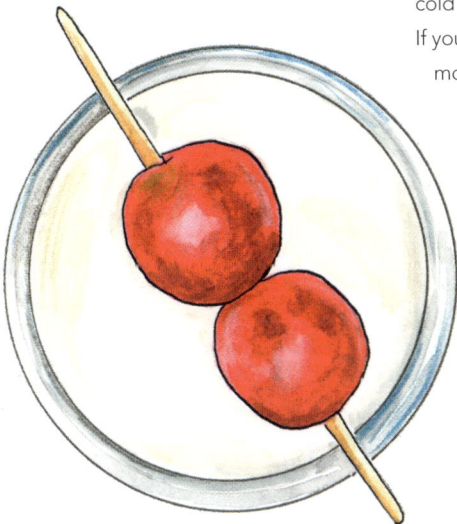

SALMOREJO

SERVES 4

Another fab cold soup originating from Andalucía in the south of Spain: a simple blend of tomatoes, old bread, olive oil and garlic.

500g ripe tomatoes – the riper, the better

150g bread – preferably day-old bread, not fresh, and the dough only, not the crust

2 garlic cloves, peeled

120ml extra virgin olive oil

100ml water

1 tsp fine sea salt

TO GARNISH:

1 egg

50g jamón ibérico (cured ham), finely chopped

2 tsp olive oil

Put the tomatoes, bread, garlic, oil, water and salt in a blender and blend until smooth. Season to taste with more salt if you think it needs it. Refrigerate until you're ready to serve – in fact, this tastes even better the next day.

Bring a small pot of cold salted water to the boil. Carefully add the egg and boil for 9–10 minutes – the yolk needs to be hard, as it will be grated later. Set aside until it's cool enough to handle, then peel.

As this is a denser soup, we love to serve it in an espresso glass as a shot, then sprinkle the grated egg and jamón on top as a garnish with a swirl of olive oil.

BRAVA SAUCE

MAKES 200ML

Brava sauce appears on every tapa menu throughout Spain and there is no one way to make it. Just as there are thousands of tapas bars around Spain, there are also thousands of different ways to make brava sauce. This is one way that we make it.

It's called 'brava' because of its fiery spiciness, but having said that, it's never too hot. It's used to complement so many different dishes, the most famous being patatas bravas (page 40), a firm favourite.

This recipe makes 200ml of brava. When using our brava and allioli sauces on patatas bravas, we tend to use less of the brava compared to the allioli. And if we're throwing a tapas party, allioli tends to appear more at the table than brava to accompany tortilla (page 37), fritura malagueña (page 28) and pincho moruno (page 22), for example.

40ml extra virgin olive oil

15g finely chopped onion (roughly ¼ large onion)

5 garlic cloves, finely chopped

1 bay leaf

½ tsp chilli flakes

½ tsp sweet paprika

200ml passata

Heat the oil in a saucepan set over a medium heat. Add the onion, garlic, bay leaf and chilli flakes and cook for 5–8 minutes, until softened but not coloured.

Remove the pan from the heat and stir in the paprika, then set aside and allow to cool. Add the passata and mix well. This is best served cold or at room temperature, never hot.

ALL ABOUT
ALLIOLI

As Anna hails from Catalunya, we always refer to this yummy sauce as allioli, but in other parts of Spain you might see it called aioli, alioli, ajoaceite, ajiaceite or ajolio.

The name of the Catalan version, allioli, is derived from its main ingredients: garlic (all) and (i) oil (oli). Kids grow up watching their parents make this at home in an instant.

It's believed that it first appeared in Ancient Egypt, then made its way up the Mediterranean with the Romans. As you can imagine, there are centuries (and generations) of recipes that have been handed down over the years.

For best results, we always recommend ensuring all your ingredients, from the oil to the egg, even the garlic, are at room temperature. This is to avoid the sauce splitting.

It was originally made by hand in a ceramic pestle and mortar and to this day is often served to the table in this traditional yellow mortero. It's such a tradition that Anna's cousin, Eva, flipped out one time when she saw Vanessa serve altramuces in our mortero (major oversight on Vanessa's part!). The mortero is for allioli only!

Our allioli accompanies so many tapas, but it's also delish if you're planning a BBQ (a parrillada de carne). We use it too on fideuà (a traditional Catalan noodle dish) or simply on toasted bread or a baked potato. There is no end to its uses.

There are many different versions of allioli. Some make it with sunflower oil rather than olive oil or with milk instead of egg, but no matter what way you choose to make it, patience is the main ingredient. Making it the traditional way, you must add the oil little by little, drop by drop, while constantly stirring until you get that delicious smooth consistency. It's worth it!

ALLIOLI
GARLIC MAYO FOR ALL INTENTS & PURPOSES

MAKES APPROX. 500ML

This recipe makes a fair amount of allioli as we tend to use more of it in comparison to our brava sauce when making patatas bravas. Since it appears in other dishes too, it's always good to have a little more in the fridge. In this book we have it accompanying our patatas bravas (page 40), our pincho moruno (page 22) and our fritura malagueña (page 28), but it's also delish simply served with toasted bread (see the pa am tomàquet on page 34).

1 large egg, at room temperature

3 garlic cloves, roughly chopped

a pinch of fine sea salt

500ml extra virgin olive oil

Crack the egg into a Pyrex jug, then add the garlic, a pinch of salt and 250ml of the olive oil. Blend until nice and smooth.

Now this is the hard part. You may find that you need to try this a few times as it can be tricky, but don't despair. While still blending (don't stop!), slowly – very slowly, little by little – we're talking drop by drop here – add the rest of the oil. The key words here are *very slowly* so as not to 'break' the allioli.

Keep blending until it's all combined. If it does split, start again. You'll eventually get it! Promise.

POSTRES
DESERTS

As we mentioned before, when it comes to bread (page 32), you can tell how important it is by the number of bakeries on each street in Spain. The same goes for anything sweet. There's a huge dessert tradition in Spain and families pass down recipes from generation to generation. They're sacrosanct.

As with traditional dishes like stews, rice and soups, each region in Spain has its own take on desserts. Not only that, but they have desserts specific to different seasons, religious celebrations and their own city, town or village festivals.

A good example is the Roscón de Reyes (kings' cake). In Spain, we celebrate the Three Kings on the 6th of January and no house is without a Roscón de Reyes. If you find the faba (bean) you pay for the tart; if you get the king figurine, you get all the luck for the year. It's a little like the charms in our barmbrack in Ireland, where the ring means you'll wed, the pea means you won't, the coin brings you wealth and the piece of cloth foretells poverty. At least the Roscón is a little more forgiving!

Here, our crema catalana (page 57) hails from Catalunya, our Tarta de Santiago (page 62) from Galicia and our arroz con leche (page 59) comes from Asturias.

Ask any Spaniard about our churros (page 60) and they'll question why they're included in the dessert section. That's because churros are traditionally served for breakfast in Spain, generally from 5 a.m. onwards – the perfect snack on your way home from the nightclub! In Lola, we serve them as a dessert. Our friends and family back home in Spain think we're mad, but they've been our most popular dessert on the menu since day one.

CREMA CATALANA

SERVES 4–6

A classic dessert. Sometimes comparisons are made with the French, who do a version called crème brûlée. But the latter is baked, whereas the catalana is made on top of the stove, and as far as some historians are concerned, crema catalana was the first to appear on the culinary scene! It's an historical snippet we always share with our customers in Las Tapas de Lola – it always creates great debate.

1 litre cold milk

40g cornflour

125g caster sugar, plus extra to caramelise

5 medium egg yolks

1 cinnamon stick

peel of 1 lemon (take care not to use any of the white part, as it's too bitter)

Put 300ml of the cold milk in a bowl with the cornflour and stir until the cornflour is completely dissolved.

In a separate bowl, mix the sugar and egg yolks together, then add this mixture to the milk and stir well to combine. Set aside.

Put the rest of the milk in a small pot with the cinnamon stick and the lemon peel. Bring to a simmer, then remove the pot from the heat, cover with a tight-fitting lid or a piece of foil and leave to infuse for 30 minutes.

Remove the cinnamon and lemon peel, then add the cornflour, sugar and egg yolk mixture.

Place the pot back on a low heat, stirring constantly until the mixture starts to thicken. After 3–4 minutes, pour the crema into small clay cazuelas or ramekins. Put in the fridge for a couple hours to set.

To serve, sprinkle a thin layer of sugar on top and caramelise it with a kitchen blowtorch.

Arroz con leche

Crema catalana

ARROZ CON LECHE
RICE PUDDING

SERVES 6–10
(depending on whether you serve it in cazuelas, ramekins or bowls)

Arroz con leche is best served cold. We've been known to steal a spoonful or two of this straight from the fridge at home! What's great is you can make it in advance, plate it and have it ready to go at the end of your party. Just dust it with ground cinnamon before serving.

2 litres full-fat milk

280g short grain rice

250g caster sugar

2 cinnamon sticks

peel of 1 lemon
(take care not to use
any of the white part,
as it's too bitter)

ground cinnamon, for
dusting

Put all the ingredients except the ground cinnamon in a heavy-based pot set over a low heat. Cook for 1½ hours. Don't allow it to boil – just keep it at a gentle simmer on a low heat and give the pot a little shake every 20 minutes to ensure it's not sticking.

Once cooked, remove the cinnamon sticks and lemon rind. Divide between cazuelas, ramekins or bowls and chill in the fridge.

Serve cold with a sprinkle of ground cinnamon on top.

CHURROS CON CHOCOLATE

SERVES 4

You'll find churrerías all over Spain serving delish churros with unctuous chocolate sauce for dipping. Typically a morning snack, we've been serving them as a dessert in Lola since day one – and they've proven to be our most popular dessert at that.

2 litres sunflower or vegetable oil, to deep-fry

250g plain flour

250ml water

1 tsp fine sea salt

2 tbsp (roughly 35g) granulated sugar, to sprinkle on top

FOR THE CHOCOLATE SAUCE:

200g chocolate (72% cocoa solids), chopped

200ml milk

Heat the oil in a deep-fryer to 190°C (see the note on page 17 if you don't have a deep-fryer).

Put the flour in a large heatproof bowl.

Put the water and salt in a pot and bring to the boil. Once the water has boiled, add it to the flour and stir with a wooden or plastic spoon until smooth.

It's easier to pipe the dough while it's still hot, so working quickly, put the dough in a piping bag fitted with a 2cm diameter star-shaped nozzle to give that lovely shape to the churros. Pipe out churros that are 10–12cm long. In churrerías in Spain, you'll see their teams pipe the churros directly into the hot oil to fry. There's a lot of skill involved in that, so at home we recommend piping them from the piping bag onto a baking tray lined with parchment paper so they don't stick, ready to fry.

Working in batches, deep-fry the churros for 2–3 minutes, until golden brown. Transfer to a plate lined with kitchen paper to absorb any excess oil.

To make the chocolate sauce, put the chocolate and milk in a saucepan set over a medium heat. Cook for 5 minutes, stirring occasionally, until the chocolate has melted and the sauce is smooth.

To serve, pour the chocolate sauce into a cup or ramekin. Pile your hot churros up on a plate (or plates). Dust the churros with granulated sugar and dip away!

TOP TIP

You can make your churros the day before – or even a week before and freeze them. They can be cooked from frozen too, though in that case they'll take 5–6 minutes to fry.

TARTA DE SANTIAGO
ALMOND TART

SERVES 8

Tarta de Santiago comes all the way from Galicia in northern Spain. It dates back as far as the Middle Ages with links, of course, to the Camino de Santiago. It's a fabulous gluten-free almond dessert, traditionally dusted with icing sugar on top with the outline of the cross of St James. You can download the traditional Tarta de Santiago stencil from the internet to decorate your tart at home.

As with so many other gastronomic traditions in Spain, in May 2010 the EU gave the Tarta de Santiago PGI (Protected Geographical Indication) status within Europe, stating, among other criteria, that the tarta mix must contain at least 33% almonds.

It's delicious served with a chilled glass of Pedro Ximénez (sweet sherry). Some like to sip it while enjoying their slice of tart, others like to pour it over the tart. Delicious either way.

butter, for greasing

6 eggs

1 tbsp amaretto

250g caster sugar

250g ground almonds

45g whole almonds, roughly crushed

zest of 1 lemon

icing sugar, for dusting

Preheat the oven to 160°C (140°C fan). Grease a 25cm cake tin with butter, paying particular attention to the sides.

In a bowl or jug, beat the eggs with the amaretto.

In a separate large bowl, mix together the sugar, ground almonds, crushed almonds and lemon zest, then add the egg mixture. Combine well, but don't beat.

Pour the batter into the greased cake tin. Bake in the preheated oven for 30 minutes, until a skewer inserted into the middle of the cake comes out clean. Remove from the oven and allow to cool completely before removing the cake from the tin, otherwise it will break apart.

Put your Tarta de Santiago stencil (see the intro) on the centre of the tart, then dust the whole tart with icing sugar. This looks great sitting on your table before slicing.

To serve, cut into eight slices and serve at room temperature. Don't forget your bottle of Pedro Ximénez for your friends!

SANGRÍA

SERVES 5

Early Greeks and Romans mixed their wine with sugar, spices and whatever was on hand. It was called hippocras and was sometimes heated, like a mulled wine. No sangría is the same. Each family has their own twist to their recipe and the best sangría is homemade. We make ours to our Cabrera family recipes.

To make any of these sangrías, simply put all the ingredients in a 1.5-litre carafe or jug and stir. Fill the carafe or jug with ice to the top, then pour into wine glasses to serve.

1 TINTO (RED WINE)

500ml red wine
300ml Club Lemon
300ml Club Orange
70ml dark rum
70ml red vermouth
½ green apple, cut into chunks
½ orange, cut into chunks (skin on)

2 BLANCO (WHITE WINE)

400ml white wine
1 x 330ml can of 7up
150ml orange juice
70ml vodka
70ml white vermouth
35ml Cointreau
35ml peach liqueur
½ green apple, cut into chunks
5 strawberries, cut into chunks

3 CAVA

500ml cava
1 x 330ml can of 7up
35ml Cointreau
35ml brandy
½ green apple, cut into chunks
½ orange, cut into chunks (skin on)

4 REBUJITO (A SHERRY TWIST)

450ml sherry
1 x 330ml can of 7up
250ml sparkling water
1 large handful of fresh mint
¼ cucumber, thinly sliced

INDEX

Nine Bean Rows
23 Mountjoy Square
Dublin, D01 E0F8
Ireland
@9beanrowsbooks
ninebeanrowsbooks.com

NINE
BEAN
ROWS

Blasta Books is an imprint of Nine Bean Rows Books Ltd.
@blastabooks blastabooks.com

First published 2023

Text Copyright © Anna Cabrera and and Vanessa Murphy, 2023

Illustrations copyright © Nicky Hooper, 2023

ISBN: 978-1-9993799-6-4

Editor: Kristin Jensen

Series artist: Nicky Hooper
nickyhooper.com

Designer: Jane Matthews
janematthews.ie

Proofreader: Jocelyn Doyle

Printed by L&C Printing Group, Poland

The paper in this book is produced using pulp from managed forests.

About the authors

For **Anna Cabrera**, food is her life. Her passion for food dates back to cooking in the kitchen with her grandmother and mother and working in her aunt's bar as a kid in Spain.

Vanessa Murphy had always dreamed of opening a tapas bar. From as far back as her early years as a child on holidays with her mum and dad in Spain, she loved running in and out of the bars on the beaches, helping the waiters to serve. Born, bred and buttered in Dublin, she studied Spanish many years ago in Trinity College and has spent over 30 years travelling to and from Spain in search of the perfect tapa.

As locals to the Wexford Street–Camden Street area in Dublin, their plan was to open a place that they would like to visit with their own friends and families – to create an atmosphere that's inviting, fun and down to earth. Their restaurant, Las Tapas de Lola, is a place where people can feel at home, relax and enjoy their food.

🖸 @lastapasdelola

🖸 @lagorditadublin